NOTHING BUT THE TRUTH

Precious memories

Pastor Deborah C. Dallas

authorHOUSE®

AuthorHouse™
1663 Liberty Drive
Bloomington, IN 47403
www.authorhouse.com
Phone: 1 (800) 839-8640

Published by AuthorHouse 06/28/2017

ISBN: 978-1-5246-7324-6 (sc)
ISBN: 978-1-5246-7323-9 (e)

FROM THE AUTHOR

I dedicate this book, first and foremost to the Most High God, my Lord and Savior, Jesus Christ. Without Him I am nothing and can't do anything. Every word written in this book is not about me, but the Power of the Holy Ghost for giving me the wisdom and strength to allow these written words to manifest and resurrect into the hearts of all those who believe in the good times; the bad times; the dark times; through emotional, spiritual, and mental breakdowns; good choices; bad choices; yet you can say right at this moment, I may have been locked down — but because of God's grace — I was never locked out!

These poems originated from the many times of struggling in this life when a sermon preached was not enough, a choir singing could not touch my pain, a prayer did not break those emotional chains, I had to realize that it's all about building a relationship with God and until we truly surrender — we will always be labeled as the Great Pretender.

To my mother, Missionary Delores C. Jones, who went home to be with the Lord 15 years ago, my armor bearer; my strength; my best friend. She was everything that a loving, saved, sanctified, Holy Ghost filled mother could be. Yes, I was my mother's only child, she

birthed me twice. Thank you mom, for placing me into the arms of God, who you always knew and believed would take care of me even when you had to say goodbye. This book would have never been written, had she not walked in obedience to God. She is my Holy Ghost filled mother who asked me to come to church with her, one Friday night May 9, 1975. I was reluctant and had other plans. I told her yes, but I was not staying. Well, it was on this night that my life changed from a "church going sinner" to a "Holy Ghost" believer. I'm talking about a life — changing power, electrifying anointing; cloven tongues of fire and deliverance!! This was not my plan. Nine months later, God called me into the ministry. He gave me a ministry of not only compassion and deliverance, but a naked and not ashamed ministry; just plain old reality, for people to know and believe that there is power in the Name of Jesus. Let me share this with you, my readers, that nobody can tell your story; that you no longer have to keep going through the motions of giving mouth-to- mouth resuscitation to a dead thing; they never saw your silent tears, nor your inward fears; now you can declare and decree in the Name of Jesus to all your haters- that although they tried to write your obituary; they even tried to pull the plug on your life; it looked like you had stopped breathing – yet they still can't understand why your heart is still beating!!

DEDICATION

This book is dedicated to my dear precious mother, Delores C. Jones, who is with the Lord. It is because of you, mother, that this book of life will begin a journey of true deliverance for many who will hunger and thirst after righteousness. Also, to my dear father, Jeremiah Jones, Jr. who is with the Lord and has always been there for me. Thank you, Jesus, for blessing me with the best parents, ever!!!

I would like to give a special thanks and heart felt gratitude to my husband, Elder Robert Dallas, who gave me the motivation to never give up on this vision. Thank you, Monique, Lamont, Jeremiah, Markia and Micah, my precious children, for allowing me to fulfill God's will for my life as you, so many times stood on the side lines to share me with the church. I want you to know that you are my greatest gifts from God. Always remember that you are strong, smart, anointed, appointed, molded and shaped by the Powerful hands of God. In each of you, there is a ministry that has been birthed. You are better than blessed. Continue to yield yourselves to the Lord as He uses you in a mighty way. Keep on the whole armor; fight the good fight of faith as you are clothed with **NOTHING BUT THE TRUTH!!**

I deeply appreciate the Whosoever Will Deliverance Temple, Inc., the most loving and supportive congregation that any pastor could ever serve. I love you.

To my Pastoral Aide. You are precious to me. Thank you for lifting up my hands and carrying me when my burdens seemed so heavy to bear.

Words cannot express my gratitude for the wisdom and mentoring I have received from the most profound preachers of the 20th century; who have stimulated seeds of greatness in my life. To Bishop Wilbur Watson, Pastor Gladys Burton Hairston and Apostle James R. Jones; I truly benefited from your anointing as I sat under you and looked up to you. To my publishing team, Elder Monique Waithe, Bro. Wilbert Thompson, Sis. Telsha Claggett and Sis. Lydia Yarborough; God has blessed my life with your obedience. You saw the magnitude of the vision, even before I did. Thank you for pushing me forward with your prayers. Words cannot express my appreciation for the countless hours you spent helping me to transform my thoughts, words, scribbles and ideas for this book, which will bless lives for years to come! You have truly understood that servant hood is essential to great leadership.

Finally, I give my Awesome, Holy, Anointed God all praise, glory and honor for the guidance of the Holy Ghost in writing this book. Without Jesus, I can do nothing. Father, you breathed in me, 42 years ago, your breath and I became a living soul to deliver your Word to people from all walks of life to speak **NOTHING BUT THE TRUTH** ! I love you Jesus!

INTRODUCTION

People write poetry every day. They <u>speak</u> it; they <u>write</u> it; they <u>sing</u> it; they hear it; they <u>dance</u> to it. I asked God to give me not just a book of poems but words of healing; words that reach the most <u>darkest</u> and <u>deepest</u> parts of my <u>readers;</u> especially those who are in <u>emotional</u>, <u>mental</u> and <u>spiritual</u> pain. Those who have sat in the church, listened to many sermons that for years were taught from preachers that we are supposed to feel spiritually fulfilled- yet we leave God's House- <u>Empty!</u>

We sing, "… the Jesus in me Loves the Jesus in you…," yet the Love we manifest is <u>conditional.</u> Love, based on my gender, my addictions, my past, my choices, my silent tears, or my assumed backslidden heart. You, my precious readers, are not holding this book by coincidence but God wants you to know and believe that at the end of the day, you are not only loved unconditionally, regardless of what others have shaped you to be when all else fails- <u>You Matter!!</u>

Heartbroken, bruised, wounded, misunderstood; emotionally hurt; can't seem to get it together; feeling like "a nobody". Guess what? — it is time for God to <u>revive</u> in you, that what has died in <u>you!</u> May these words of life, bring healing to those who are wounded, bruised and broken.

'Cuz ain't nobody mad but the devil'

FOREWORD

In a day when so many of us in the Body of Christ and those of us outside the will of God are experiencing tremendous attack and persecution from the enemy, very few books strike the reader as a tool to heal what is sick in them and to revive what has died in them. These are not poems written just to fill in your time. Please know that I take no credit for these words written. These poems were sent by God through Holy Ghost inspiration. If you read this Heaven-sent Word with an open mind; you will find yourself in this book because God's Word will not return to Him void. Yes, your pain is real as well as the spiritual conflict that you struggle against. You can survive with Jesus on your side! Remember that your most important defense against adversity is recognizing the enemy and knowing how to defeat him.

A NOTE FROM THE CHURCH FAMILY

Pastor Dallas does not, in any way, shape or form, sugar coat the Word of God to satisfy the fleshly desires of this life. She speaks nothing but the truth. Knowing that as much as the truth hurts; it also will heal!

Sometimes, you must hurt in order to <u>know</u>; fall in order to grow; lose in order to <u>gain</u> because most of Life's greatest lessons are learned through <u>pain</u>. Galatians 6:9 – And let us not be weary in well-doing for in due season, we shall reap, if we faint not.

The blessing of these poems lies in the encouragement you will receive as you realize that all of your power and answers are in the <u>Name of Jesus!</u> Pastor Dallas has been ordained by God to help us to become better equipped to handle the adversity that is sure to come.

Lovingly submitted by the Church Family
of the Whosoever Will Deliverance Temple, Inc.

WHEN JESUS WAS FIRST
PART I

One time you were so faithful in reading God's word,

You had days set aside that you Hungered and Thirst!!!

But 0' that was when Jesus was First!!

No phone calls, nor home visits were permitted,

For unto Jesus your life was committed.

0' remember that special time you waited as you sat in the chair,

For there was so much with Jesus you wanted to share.

As you felt His presence come into the room,

You said, "Hello JESUS, 0' How I Love You!!!"

You embraced Him in His love, as tears of JOY ran down your face,

Knowing that this was your Only Friend and your Special Place.

There was nothing that you had to hide,

Because you knew that your heart was opened wide.

O' So many times you told Him that He was the Lover of your Soul,

But one day later your Love turned cold.

Jesus kept His Promise, and He always showed up at that place,

He called and searched for you, because He did not understand,

How one day you decided to Let Go of His Hand.

But now you have deserted Him, and gone away to stay,

Jesus cried with tears in His eyes and said, "What did I do," or "What

did I say," to make you treat me this way?

Remember our Promise to never depart, and now you've left me with

a Broken Heart.

WHEN JESUS WAS FIRST
PART II

Can't you see tears in my eyes?

I am even willing to apologize.

Can't you see, you are the one for me.

You left me empty with no Explanation,

Don't you remember that I Am Salvation?

Yes, your love for me, satan has stole,

But I am the one who died for your soul.

Come back, my Love, don't hurt me anymore

Satan is a Counterfeit, but My Love is SURE!!!

Read my Word, study it day and night,

This is the only way that you can win the Fight.

You used to fast and pray with no number in mind,

You won souls to for me, because your spirit was kind.

You took a stand before your family,

And testified to how I set you free.

I hurt, and I Thirst for your love once again,

But now you've left me for sin and shame!!

One time it would have mattered when you knew that I was hurt,

But 0' I forgot, that was only, WHEN JESUS WAS FIRST!!!

THE INWARD FIGHT

When you truly give JESUS your life, then you will lose your Inward Fight.

The only time you find yourself opposing, is when you have if, ands, buts and supposings.

When your mind is made up to serve the Lord, then your spirit concerning holiness will be on one accord.

You're not deceiving anyone but yourself, when you denied the word, and chose to rebel:

Deep down within, you really didn't feel that it was a sin!

Time will tell what you really surrendered from the heart that is true, when the spirit of rebellion began to rise in you!

All you give to JESUS is over, done with and out of your life.
All that you hold on to becomes that INWARD FIGHT!

SEE YOURSELF

Many times throughout this life,

It seem like nothing is going right.

The Harder we try,

The more we cry.

It's time to *see* yourself,

In the eyes of the LORD!

Be disconnected from Satan's unbiblical cord.

What you will see in you,

Will want you to think, that's not TRUE!

We all would like to be better than what we are,

But face reality about the real you,

And say there is something "I MUST DO".

Stop trying so hard to make others smile, and concentrate on being

God's Holy Child.

You were not only created to bring to others JOY and PEACE,

But JESUS also came to keep you FREE!

Many years you've cried so many tears, but JESUS came to erase ALL your Fears!

You are human, and not a piece of STEEL, and GOD cares exactly how you feel!!!

See yourself, don't close your eyes, JESUS knew all you tried to hide. He only came to make you be, better than what you really SEE!!

WHEN YOU ARE HALF-DRESSED;
YOU WILL FAIL THE TEST

Everybody wants to be a soldier, but don't want to fight.

Always crying LORD make me stronger, but you won't put on the whole armour.

You can't go into battle with what you think is best, all that you will do, is fail the test!

0' you know when you are half-dressed because you have no joy in your life. Not only that, but Satan has put out your sight!

The things you need to see, you can't see no more, because you are trying to enter in every other way, when JESUS, is the TRUE DOOR!

God's soldiers don't get weak, because they are HOLY GHOST filled and complete.

You can't STAND when you reject God's COMMAND!

You just can't wear grace, and don't put on faith.

Neither can you just put on works, and reject the BLOOD washed church.

Stop crying LORD make me stronger, and just put on the whole armour.

The whole armour is the HOLY GHOST, you either put on that which God has required, or ye shall surely die!

WHEN YOUR WEIGHTS ARE
SET ASIDE - THE NAME OF
JESUS YOU WILL MAGNIFY

It's time to stop sitting in church living a LIE, you have not yet put your weights aside.

Acting like you are sanctified, yet the name of JESUS you cannot Magnify!

Holy people the Rapture is near, keep praising the LORD in godly fear.

Get ready to meet JESUS and do it today, in the twinkling of an eye - we shall be caught up and taken away!

When you stop acting like you trust Him when all the time you sit in doubt, magnifying the LORD will be the only way OUT!

Sitting in the church bored as can be, trying to act like you got the Victory.

On your tree, you ain't got nothing but leaves, no wonder you can't stay free.

But the Holy people got fruit on their trees and they can truly Shout the VICTORY!!

BAAL OR THE BLOOD STAINED NAILS

Don't bow to Baal, but remember the BLOOD STAINED NAILS.!!!

JESUS NEVER FAILS!!!!

Just hold out a little while longer, JESUS promised to make you stronger!

The FLESH is weak and want to give up, but just remember WHO drank from the BITTER CUP!

Satan is here to bring Temptation, but it was JESUS, who died to give us SALVATION!!

Concentrate on the ONE who endured your pain, then you won't find any room to COMPLAIN!!

JUST LIFT UP YOUR VOICE AND, PRAISE JESUS NAME!!

TORN BETWEEN FILTHY AND CLEAN!

It comes a time in each and every one of our

lives, that we must make a choice, whether or not we will obey God's

Voice!

JESUS doesn't want you by force,

He wants you to make a Choice.

Get rid of your two lovers, crying to one lover, while you make love

to the other.

You can't LOVE the world and Holiness at the same time.

Stop trying to serve (2) two, thinking that JESUS don't see all that

you do!

For GOD said "I saw you when you did it, and you never REPENTED!

Stop trying to be a lay member and a Pastor at the same time.

Stay in your calling and stay out of the business of everybody else, then you will have more time to concentrate on yourself.

It's time to make a choice of what or who you want to be, "WILL IT BE HELL FIRE OR ETERNAL VICTORY?"

WHEN JESUS WAS HUNGRY

When Jesus was Hungry and came looking for
something to eat, He found you unfruitful sitting$_4$ in the same seat.

All the time, JESUS was so tired for supplying all of your needs, but
all He got in return was <NOTHING BUT LEAVES>.

JESUS SAID, "When I hungered, you gave me no meat, Just a face
filled with pity and defeat.

What did My crucifixion really mean to you, was it to change you
from OLD to NEW?

Each time I returned, you gave me sin and shame! Was my dying for
you JUST ALL IN VAIN?

0' the many prayers you prayed for me to meet your needs, but all I
got in return was <NOTHING BUT LEAVES>

Nothing but leaves, Nothing but leaves, That's what JESUS receives
for setting the captives free!

Then you wonder why you can't be a soul-winner, as long as you're cursed, you are still a sinner.

This is not the first time that JESUS has come in the garden and each time He finds your heart still HARDENED!

When JESUS curses your tree, no SPIRITUAL fruit can you bear because your only communication with God is through prayer.

THERE IS NO ROOM

Satan knows that if he can get a little anger, offense, or hypocrisy in your heart from you JESUS will DEPART.

His motive is to get you so mad at the person, that you want to fight, for the demons know to hold anger is not RIGHT!!

The devil knows that HELL is Still HOT and he knows the scripture, "BE ANGRY AND SIN NOT!"

Regardless of how evil a person is,
Don't let them bring you *down* to their level,
and after a good service they have you looking and acting like the devil!!

If you find yourself feeling ugly, edgy, and mean, it's that demon whose name is "UNCLEAN."

Don't give him strength by shutting your mouth,

Rebuke that devil and tell him that THERE IS NO ROOM IN YOUR HOUSE!

Tell him to go to somebody else that sit in the church without a testimony of Victory,

For you are no more Bound, but JESUS set you FREE!

Now you know you have something to shout about.

Just knowing that the demons wanted you to let them in, but they saw the BLOOD and remembered that you were FREE FROM ALL SIN!!!

"BACKSLIDER ON THE RUN"

Just like a fool-being used as Satan's tool! You left the Great Physician,

in exchange for some hugging and kissing.

You couldn't take the penicillin, because your

heart was not WILLING.

Trying to stay strong with your over the

counter drugs, sweeping your sins underneath the rugs.

RUN ON "BACKSLIDER"

You're just getting deeper into sin

REJECTING THE <BEGINNING> BUT YOU WILL SURELY

FACE THE [END]!!

Printed in the United States
By Bookmasters